How do I make the
next book better?

I0471429

How do I make the next book better?

David Bergsland

Radiqx PRESS

Written and published Summer, 2013
© David Bergsland • All Rights Reserved
Mankato, Minnesota • http://radiqx.com • info@radiqx.com
ISBN-13: 978-1491006436
ISBN-10: 1491006439

Adobe InDesign CC® screen shots created with permission from Adobe Systems Incorporated. Adobe®, Adobe InDesign CC® are either registered trademarks or trademarks of Adobe Systems Incorporated in the United States and/or other countries. The same applies to shots from Adobe InDesign CS5.5® & CS6® where I used screen shots from that app.

Cover art: The photo is where I work every day. The font is Contenu Book Display set narrow.

Please let us know if there is anyway I can help you in your publishing endeavors.

*This is dedicated to
the self-publishing author, like me,
with little capital and no training.*

Contents

How can I make it better the next time? ... 1
My goal is to save you money and time ... 3

Using Word for books ... 5
Fonts & the characters within ... 7
Other additional characters ... 10
OpenType abilities ... 15
Publishing instruction is typographical ... 15

Setting up your Word or word processing document ... 41
The main thing is consistency ... 42
Normal word processing issues ... 43
Here is a procedure that will eliminate most common word processor typos in a few brief steps: ... 45

Other books & resources ... 49

How can I make it better the next time?

This is the plaintive question I get every time I set up a book for a new author. It is also one of the most common questions I see in the FaceBook and Linked-In groups, Google+ communities, and specialized forums in which I spend time. It is coupled with the question, "How can I get the print version set up?"

There are three basic underlying concepts here

- Producing a print version of your book
- The size of your production budget for ebooks
- Producing a professional manuscript which can be formatted efficiently

Let's take the first concept and get it out of the way. Many new self-publishing authors writing fiction believe that they do not need a print version. You may be right. However, most of them eventually want a printed copy to give to friends; they discover an excellent reviewer who requires a printed copy; or they try to use the giveaway promotion opportunities on a site like GoodReads. Then they find themselves lost in a strange new world where everything they knew no longer works. Let's get it out in the open:

Preparing a print version of your book in Word or any other word processor is virtually impossible!

There are some good resources for those who feel compelled to try. But most of them are really bad. You do not want the help of an untrained Word user formatting your book. They'll get it working, but the professionalism needed to earn reader trust will not be there.

The best way is to buy a template from a book designer you trust. The only ones I know about come from Joel Friedlander. He's been a professional book designer for many years

2: How Can I Make It Better?

and he offers book templates for Word at very reasonable prices. I think he still gets less than $40 for a template. Try thebookdesigner.com to look at them.

How much do you want to spend on ebook production?

The second concept is also important to consider—and make decisions about. Many writers will tell you about the thousands of dollars needed to publish a book. As I recall, Guy Kawasaki in APE talks about four to five thousand dollars, and he is doing all the production himself.

Many of us do not have nearly those resources. Without money, it will take time. Publishing a book is an immensely complex project. The skillsets needed are large, and require practice and experience.

My contention is that, with study and practice, you can publish your books for free. Your only costs will be a small monthly fee for your software plus online access. In addition, you will need to learn a lot about an industry which is relatively unknown to the general public: publishing.

Some of the skill sets needed

1. Writing
2. Editing & proofing
3. Typography
4. Cover design
5. Print requirements: high quality, high resolution
6. Proper formatting for uploading: JPEGs, PNGs, & PDFs for graphics and covers. PDFs, ePUBs, & KF8 for the interior of the books.
7. Book marketing: content, genre, & niche
8. Online social networking

One of them is an area you can learn by yourself—easily. That is typography. This little book is to help you learn the basics of typography. You will quickly discover that many of the core typographic issues cannot be accomplished in Word or any other word processor.

Professional book design requires InDesign

InDesign [and QuarkXPress] are really the only software applications which are developed for professional designers. These applications are designed to do skill sets two through six in the list on the opposite page. Because they are designed to produce this work, they do it better, faster, and much more efficiently. For book design, nothing is better than InDesign. It handles skill sets one through seven.

The key skill, virtually unknown outside of graphic design, is how to present the words so they can be read effortlessly and easily understood. There is a basic level of competency which must be reached. For professional book production, you need to understand the core of professional book design: typography.

That is the purpose of this book. It will teach you the basics you need to be able to use in a professional Word template, to give your manuscript to a trained book designer, or to produce it yourself. I've written other, far more detailed books which cover the entire process from two to eight—everything other than the actual writing.

Practical Professional Self-Publishing Handbook [InDesign CC]: This book is for the professional graphic designer who wants to format books for self-publishers.

Writing In InDesign [currently at edition 2.5 for InDesign CS6]: This book is for authors who want or need to do it all themselves. There's a real joy and an incredible creative experience that comes from treating the entire book as a project creatively controlled by one artist: writer, designer, and publisher.

My goal is to save you money and time

Some of this is very practical. For example, if I discover that you know the principles talked about in this book, I cut my formatting charges to design and publish your book in half. To give you an idea of how much that means, for the textbooks I published traditionally, I made twice as much to format the books for those publishers as I did in royalties for book sales. I currently charge about 10% of what I was

4: How Can I Make It Better?

paid to format my textbooks. If you understand typography, I can cut that 10% in half.

You can pay an copyeditor to clean up the writing for you, but that can easily cost $300 to a couple thousand dollars. It still will not help solve the typographic requirements which enable you to give your readers an enjoyable reading experience.

These things are the main reasons why you only get 10% royalties or so from a traditional publisher. They are professional requirements, regardless of the production method. You choose whether you want to spend your time writing query letters, contacting agents and all of that or learning what it takes to publish your books yourself, for free.

At present, I publish several books a year. My only expenses are what I pay for online access. You can learn how to do that also.

Using Word for books

My viewpoint of Word is skewed by my experience. Most of the problems I have had over the years were problems caused by Word's inabilities. However, if you are a typical author, you have no idea about why that might be so. This little booklet is written to explain the problems and give solutions to those issues.

If all you know is Word and that not well, Word can do an adequate job for you—for ebooks. But you do need to be aware of the areas which Word [or any other word processor] cannot handle. You also need to know what is expected in a book. Many of the problems can be solved as you write. All you need to do is learn what is required.

You need to do what you can in Word to work consistently and professionally. This little book will introduce you to the changes necessary typographically in book design. It is true that some things cannot be done in Kindle books or even ePUBs because of the HTML involved in their construction. But PDFs can show it all. And print books actually require this knowledge.

The professional assumption

All book design pros know that the word processing file you wrote so carefully will be taken into InDesign [or possibly QuarkXPress] for formatting and book production. Obviously there are two problems with that. First of all, most of the new breed of self-publishing authors are going to try and produce their book directly from the Word document. Secondly, especially for fiction there may never be a print quality design.

Starting with a print version solves many difficulties in book design. Typography is added. This is the basic attribute upon which Word falls. Many of the typographic norms, which are standard in printing, are simply not possible in Word or any other word processor.

Type has nothing to do with typing.

6: How Can I Make It Better?

It is obvious that even the terminology is different. However, we have hardly begun. Much more significant than the new language are the actual mechanics of typesetting. The rules have changed! In fact, one of the difficulties in teaching publishing classes today involves a paradox. Writing classes are secretarial teaching office assistants how to produce standard business documents. But these standards are all based on typewriter abilities.

- **Classes all teach writing using Word:** but Word cannot produce professional typography or the formatting services required by the reader.
- **Writing groups assume Word:** if you give them a PDF to annotate many will freak out.
- **Learning to type in a keyboarding or word processing class teaches students so many bad habits that you wonder if it is worth it:** you'll need to train yourself how to write fully formatted.

As an author, typing skills obviously help. However, you are wasting your time and confusing the entire process if you do not learn to type, format, and edit professionally.

So, who really cares?

Actually, you do. One of the things of which most beginning designers are not aware is the extreme (but usually subconscious) distinctions between what I call secretarial or business type and professional typeset copy. You are very aware of the differences—just not on a conscious level.

You have been making decisions about companies, products, and services for years that are based, at least part, upon their perceived honesty, integrity, trustworthiness, and so on as seen in their advertising and marketing efforts. These attributes are influenced by the carefully crafted typography used in their production.

This is true in books also. Many of your readers' perceptions about your concept and content will come from reactions to type used not only inside the book, but on the cover. It is likely you cannot explain the difference at this point. However, you can tell at a glance whether something is bureaucratic, cheap, top quality, and so on by the typography.

The democratization of typography

The problem, of course, is that everyone now believes that they have the capability to produce writing—whatever that means. It is possible (to a very limited extent) in Word, and that covers almost everyone. It is very difficult to generate professional typography in a word processor though. All of this is confused by the fact that everyone has access to the same fonts, and the same basic capabilities. Most people simply do not have any idea how far typography goes beyond word processing.

Fonts & the characters within

There are many more things you need to know about typefaces. A font is simply a complete set of characters for a given style. It is available in any size from a tenth of a point to 1296 points in InDesign. Below I am showing you the font used for this book named Contenu (which I designed), showing some of the 563 characters available in it. Notice the three styles of numbers (among other things).

Contenu Book

ABCDEFGHIJKLMNOPQRSTUVWXYZ1234567
abcdefghijklmnopqrstuvwxyz1234567890
ABCDEFGHIJKLMNOPQRSTUVWXYZ1234567890
!@#$%^&*( )!@#$%^&*( )_+{}|:"<>?,./;'[]\=-
¡ ½¼¾³²¦-×~ÄÅÇÉÑÖÜáàâäãåçèéeë
í""ïñóòôöõúùûüt°¢£□•¶ß®©™¨ÆØ∞
±¥µª°æø¿¡¬ƒ≈Δ«»…ÀÃÕŒœ--""'+ÿŸ/‹fi‡·"‰
ÂÊÁËÈÍÎÏÌÓÔÒÚÛÙı˜˘˙˚¸˝˛ˇ

Hundreds of characters

However, hundreds just barely begins to cover the characters needed for typesetting. Typewriters were limited

8: How Can I Make It Better?

to about 88 characters, although that varied a little. We had the QWERTY keyboard and then those same keys with the shift key held down. The shift key was called that because it physically shifted the entire set of letters—lifting them high enough to use the second set available on all the metal keys.

Many of you still think that these are all the letters we need. This is not true. This is not even close to being correct. In fact, we need access to several hundred characters, as professional typesetters and authors. Even in English we are really limited. But first, we need to mention one of the major differences between PC and Mac.

7-bit ASCII: the PC limitation

When Bill (Gates) and the crew designed DOS, they were very pleased to offer 7-bit ASCII. ASCII is just an acronym for a regulating group setting a standard numbering order for letter characters, but the key here is 7-bit. Remembering your digital code, 7-bit is 128 choices. So, PCs had 128 characters.

8-bit ASCII: the Mac limitation

When the Mac came out, it supported 8-bit ASCII. However, even the 256 characters of 8-bit ASCII do not even come close to what is needed for typesetting.

Upper ASCII

8-bit ASCII is essential for desktop publishing. Without all 256 characters, there are many things that are a real pain. As a PC user, you will run into that pain very quickly. There are many special characters that you will need to use all the time. On a PC, these characters are called upper ASCII characters and are only available by holding down the Alt key and typing four numbers on the numerical keypad. The chart on the next page shows all 128 upper-ASCII characters. Those from 129 and up require the Alt+four-number routine. The number is in the gray bar to the right of the character the character. The code in the middle column is for the Mac keystroke: O = Option, S = Shift.

You will end up memorizing many of these special keystrokes for simple things like bullets, ™ trademark, © copyright, and ® registered characters.

Keystrokes for the upper 128 of the ASCII set
Mac & Windows shortcuts for the standard characters in most fonts

Glyph	Mac	PC: Alt+	Glyph	Mac	PC: Alt+	Glyph	Mac	PC: Alt+	Glyph	Mac	PC: Alt+
		0129	€	SO-2	0164	Ã	On-A	0195	â	OI-a	0226
,	SO-0	0130	¥	O-y	0165	Ä	Ou-A	0196	ã	On-a	0227
ƒ	O-f	0131	¦		0166	Å	SO-a	0197	ä	Ou-a	0228
„	SO-w	0132	§	O-6	0167	Æ	SO-'	0198	å	Oa	0229
…	O-;	0133	¨	SO-u	0168	Ç	SO-c	0199	æ	O'	0230
†	O-t	0134	©	O-g	0169	È	O`-E	0200	ç	Oc	0231
‡	SO-7	0135	ª		0170	É	Oe-E	0201	è	O`-e	0232
ˆ	SO-i	0136	«	O-\	0171	Ê	OI-E	0202	é	Oe-e	0233
‰	SO-r	0137	¬	O-l	0172	Ë	Ou-E	0203	ê	OI-e	0234
Š		0138			0173	Ì	O`-I	0204	ë	Ou-e	0235
‹	SO-3	0139	®	O-r	0174	Í	Oe-I	0205	ì	O`-I	0236
Œ	SO-q	0140	¯	SO-,	0175	Î	OI-I	0206	í	Oe-i	0237
		0141–0144	°	SO-8	0176	Ï	Ou-I	0207	î	OI-i	0238
'	O-]	0145	±	SO-=	0177	Ð		0208	ï	Ou-i	0239
'	SO-]	0146	²		0178	Ñ	On-N	0209	ð		0240
"	O-[	0147	³		0179	Ò	O`-O	0210	ñ	On-n	0241
"	SO-[	0148	´	SO-e	0180	Ó	Oe-O	0211	ò	O`-o	0242
•	O-8	0149	µ	O-m	0181	Ô	OI-O	0212	ó	Oe-o	0243
–	O--	0150	¶	O-7	0182	Õ	On-O	0213	ô	OI-I	0244
—	OS--	0151	·	SO-9	0183	Ö	Ou-O	0214	õ	On-n	0245
~	SO-n	0152	¸	SO-z	0184	×		0215	ö	Ou-o	0246
™	O-2	0153	¹		0185	Ø	SO-o	0216	÷	O/	0247
š		0154	º	O-0	0186	Ù	Ou-U	0217	ø	Oo	0248
›	SO-4	0155	»	SO-\	0187	Ú	Oe-U	0218	ù	O`-u	0249
œ	O-q	0156	¼		0188	Û	OI-U	0219	ú	Oe-u	0250
		0157–0158	½		0189	Ü	Ou-U	0220	û	OI-u	0251
Ÿ	Ou-Sy	0159	¾		0190	Ý		0221	ü	Ou-u	0252
		0160	¿	SO-?	0191	Þ		0222	ý		0253
¡	O-1	0161	À	O`-A	0192	ß	Os	0223	þ		0254
¢	O-4	0162	Á	Oe-A	0193	À	O`-a	0224	ÿ	Ou-y	0255
£	O-3	0163	Â	OI-A	0194	á	Oe-a	0225			0256

≤ ≥ Ω ✦ ≈ π ∏ ∑ √ ∫ ≠ These Option characters are not available on a PC. On a PC, hold down the Alt key and type the ASCII number on the numerical keypad. The blank Mac keys are Control characters not normally available. **For a Mac, S = Shift and O = Option.**
For Mac composite characters like Ö [Option+U then the O], you type the combination to access the accent [which remains invisible] and then type the letter you want the character to appear over — at which point the accented character will be typed.

A service of Radiqx Press

An easier to read, free, letter sized version is available as a PDF at Scribd.com—http://www.scribd.com/doc/15594280/Keystroke-Table

10: How Can I Make It Better?

The cross-platform issues

In early desktop publishing this was a major issue. Not only were PCs 7-bit and Macs 8-bit, but PCs could not read Mac fonts and Macs could not read PC fonts. InDesign solved this problem. Word never did. OpenType solved the problems. We'll mention this OpenType solution after we look at some special characters. But Word cannot use it and neither can ePUBs or Kindle books.

Other additional characters

Small caps

One of the typesetting options in most professional software (and many word processors) has been the use of small caps. Most of you are probably familiar with this from tutorials of any of the professional publishing programs. Small caps are capital letters that have been reduced to the x-height and used in place of lower case letters.

Small Caps

10:07 AM or July 24, 11:15 PM

USA 1776 or USA 1776 or USA 1776

United Nations UNESCO for AIDS along with the FBI, CIA, NSA, plus the cops of EuroPol

The problem is that you may have never seen true small caps. WHAT WE NORMALLY GET IS PROPORTIONALLY REDUCED CAPS. THIS MAKES SMALL CAPS LOOK MUCH THINNER AND LIGHTER THAN THE CAPITALS THEY ARE WITH. WITH TRUE SMALL CAPS, THE STROKE WEIGHTS OF THE SMALL CAPS ARE THE SAME AS FOR THE CAPS AND LOWERCASE OF THE NORMAL FONT. There are quite a few specialized fonts that have no lowercase – just caps and small caps. There isn't room to fit true small caps into an 8-bit (256 character) font that already has lowercase letters.

Old style figures

In the printed book, some of you might have noticed that the numbers used in the body copy of this book seem to flow with the type a little better than usual. That is because the font I am using has old style figures. Most of you probably think that numbers are always the same height and width. These are called lining figures. Actually, I tend to call them bookkeepers' numbers, because I think that is the only place to use them. But that is another story. For Contenu Book, the font used here, the numbers are supposed to have 1,2,& 0 at the x-height; 3, 4, 5, 7, & 9 with descenders; and 6 & 8 with ascenders – oldstyle figures instead of the lining figures. In fact, because it is one of my OpenType fonts I have the choice of Lining, Oldstyle, and Small Cap figures [figures the same size and weight as the small caps].

Oldstyle figures: 1234567890
LINING FIGURES: 1234567890
SMALL CAP FIGURES: 1234567890

Lining figures are appropriate for use with capital letters and in financial tables, but nothing else. In fact, they look like capitalized characters in the flow of regular C&lc copy. Oldstyle figures are far less intrusive and flow much better when reading. Small Cap figures are used with small caps. They flow so much better that it is likely that many of you didn't even notice that I was using them until I just mentioned it. There isn't room to fit oldstyle figures into an 8-bit font that already has lining figures [& certainly not Small Cap figures]. Because ebooks do not support OpenType (except for PDFs) you always get those horrible lining figures in your books. I finally made a special version called Contenu eBook with oldstyle figures to work with ebooks.

Ligatures

In some cases, letters simply do not fit very well. The typographic solution has been to make special composite characters where two or more letters are made into one character that looks better. In Gutenberg's 42-line Bible, since justification hadn't been invented yet, he used over 3,000 ligatures to help justify his copy. However, through the years, ligatures have been essential to the beauty of the type. Again, the problem has been the 256-character limit.

The Lord is my Shepherd; I shall not want.

He makes me to lie down in green pastures;
He leads me beside the still waters.

He restores my soul; He leads me in the paths
of righteousness for His name's sake.

Yea, though I walk through the valley
of the shadow of death,
I will fear no evil; for You are with me;
Your rod and Your staff, they comfort me.
You prepare a table before me
in the presence of my enemies;
You anoint my head with oil; my cup runs over.
Surely goodness and mercy shall follow me
all the days of my life; and I will dwell
in the house of the Lord forever.

As usual, the problem is that only the 8-bit characters are available in Kindle with the embedded fonts. So, even if I wanted to use them, they are not available.

Swashes

With some of the old fonts, especially those that mimicked handwriting, specialized character variants were created to add grace and style to the type. These swashes also were lost when we went to the 256-character limit.

In the graphic to the left on the opposite page, you see the twenty-third psalm set in Caflisch Script Pro from Adobe. This font has many dozens of swashes and ligatures added automatically. Especially notice the k in the word walk in "Yea, though I walk through the valley" in the middle of the psalm when compared to the k in maketh (the third line). This swash at the end of the word was added automatically by the font. Also notice the d in goodness compared to the d in days (the 3rd and 2nd lines from the bottom of the psalm).

Fractions, numerators, denominators, superiors, and inferiors

To typesetters, fractions are a real problem. Most PC fonts have ½, ¼, ¾ plus $^{1\,2\,3}$. But, what do you do about 61/64 or something like that? In reality, that should look more like this $^{61}/_{64}$. But again that only works when you have an OpenType font with Numerators and Denominators. There isn't room to fit fractions, numerators, denominators, superiors, and inferiors into an 8-bit font—or any of the options individually for that matter.

Cut studs to 89$^{13}/_{64}$"

Superscript and subscript

These are conceptually the same as superiors and inferiors except that they apply to all the caps, lower case, and numbers. The most common place you see them is in mathematical and chemical formulas.

14: How Can I Make It Better?

An algebraic expression might be something like this: a^3+b^4. A chemical formula might look like this: NO_2. This type of thing obviously does not work very well with oldstyle figures. It's a little better with lining figures [a^3+b^4 & N_2O_3] though they still need fixing by moving figures up and down. The problem with this is the same as with true small caps: these characters need to be designed smaller but with the same stroke weight so they look like they fit. Plus, by now you know there simply isn't room to fit all the superscript and subscript characters into an 8-bit, 256 character font.

Italics and Obliques

In Italy in the early Renaissance—in Venice, a man named Aldus Manutius developed a font based on the handwriting of his day, which he called *Italic*. It became very popular, but because of the narrowness and tight fit of the letters, it was not as legible — and still isn't. Italics were completely separate fonts and they were not used on the same page as roman fonts until the pomp and ebullience of the Baroque.

In this day and age, every normal vertical style has a matching italic — Contenu Book Regular, *Contenu Book Italic*. As you can clearly see in these six words, italic is a very different font. The *a*, *n*, and *l* show the most obvious differences. With some fonts, the matching of these two type styles is done very well and elegantly. In other cases, the two fonts are seemingly just forced into the same bed.

One of the aberrations of the digital age is a new phenomenon of fake italics called *oblique*. These are not true italics, but merely slanted roman characters. This is not a true italic. Obliques have been known to drive type purists nuts (but for most of them it's just a short putt anyway)!

Studying *Studying*

Here's a comparison of oblique & italic in Garamond

OpenType abilities

This relatively new font format [in the new millennium] solves most of these problems. InDesign was the first professional application to use the format. The Creative Suite or Cloud is about the only place where they are in constant use. They do not work in word processors. OpenType is completely cross-platform. For the first time you can use the same fonts on a Mac and on a PC. But the new format goes far beyond that.

So, what does it do?

First, it completely solves the number of characters limitation. OpenType fonts can have over 65,000 characters. Few do, but they can, if needed. What this means on a practical level is that almost all of the options we have talked about are available (or can be made available) automatically in InDesign as you write: oldstyle figures, optical scaling, true small caps, inferior and superior characters, automatic building of true fractions, ligatures, swashes, plus Greek and Cyrillic alphabets. All of these are optional settings in InDesign paragraph and character styles. **But they do not work in ePUBs or Kindle books.**

Publishing instruction is typographical

Now we are going to talk about basic things that you must add to your writing style. Many of these things run contrary to what you were taught when you learned to type. This is especially true if you ever took a typing course. You will find you have many things to unlearn.

1. **No double spacing**

    Typing classes teach that one should always double-space after punctuation. This was made necessary by the typewriter characters themselves. All characters on a typewriter are the same width. This is called a monospaced typeface. The result is that punctuation becomes hard to see. The double space emphasizes sentence construction and makes it visible.

16: How Can I Make It Better?

When you are using monospaced fonts, this type of extra spacing is necessary. You can see an example of the horrors of monospaced type below.

Typesetting, in contrast, is done with proportional type. This means that every character has its own width that is designed to fit with the other characters. Typeset words form units characterized by even spacing between every letter. In fact, professional typesetting is judged by this smooth type color, as we just discussed. Double-spacing is not needed because the better-fitting words make punctuation a major break. In addition, there is extra white space built into the typeset punctuation characters themselves. Double-spacing after punctuation puts little white holes in the type color. These speckled paragraphs are not nearly so elegant, beautiful, or clear.

```
If you look at this paragraph
closely, you will see that the
spacing looks far different from the
paragraphs above and below. It is
set in Courier, which is a
monospaced font. As you can see,
the spacing is horrible. Much of
this is because of the letter shapes
themselves. But the main problem is
that all characters have the same
width — including spaces and
punctuation. As a result, everything
lines up vertically. This is what
monospacing means.
```

In the sample above, the paragraph in Courier was a real pain to typeset: There are so many automatic controls in InDesign that the monospaced characters would not line up correctly. I had to make a separate text block and turn off all the controls to make this demo. Even yet, the monospacing has been modified a little to make it work like typewriter type.

This double-spacing typing rule is taught even though most people using word processors have not used monospaced type for years. The rule is just taught because "We have always done it that way."

2. No double returns [HORRIBLE PARAGRAPH SPACING]

Spacing between the paragraphs is not done with the Return key: It is done with the Space Before and Space After fields in your Paragraph settings. The extra space between paragraphs helps the lines of type in the paragraph hold together in a unit. It is especially important to do this in bulleted lists where the paragraphs are short – two or three lines.

The reason for this is that spacing in typography uses adjustments that are so small, you cannot control them by eye. Although you can clearly see the relationships, hand-adjusted consistency is impossible on a 72 dpi monitor because most of the adjustments are less than a point—or smaller than a pixel. You can only adjust type relative to itself in increments of small portions of a point.

The first place you will run across this dilemma in our current discussion is with paragraph spacing. Space between paragraphs is controlled with the space before paragraph and space after paragraph options—not with multiple returns. Just remember that in most cases, zero is best as you see in this paragraph.

Spacing helps to communicate, it doesn't just make a pretty page.

Double return problems

How should we set up our paragraph spacing? First, be aware that double returns add huge, horizontal white bars that run across your pages—disrupting type color. When cleaning up word processor copy, you will regularly come across multiple returns—maybe a dozen or more. This is because most secretaries have no clue about the flow of copy. These things are not taught in word processing classes. So they simply type multiple returns to get to the next page.

You want to establish a rhythm to your pages that makes the paragraphs easy to see without being obvious. A couple of points before or after each paragraph is enough. If you do not use a first-line indent, you will probably need to use four to seven points before or after your paragraphs. Try to use as little extra spacing as possible while still making your structure easy to follow while reading. To keep it consistent, this spacing needs to be built into your paragraph styles. Then you can control it globally as your sense of style develops through the writing of your book.

For headlines and subheads, their positioning is controlled to a large degree by the space before and the space after a paragraph. You want more space before a header and less after so the header is tied to the copy that follows. For this reason, I sometimes use a couple of points after my body copy paragraphs to help with the lead-in space to the next paragraph style—especially headers.

3. Space, space and a half, or double space?

None of the above! This is why we use leading instead of spacing. Space is old typewriter terminology. The three options listed above were the only ones available for typewriters. In almost every case (unless you are trying to mimic a typewriter) a single space is too close, a space and a half is too far, and a double space is ridiculous. Again, the focus has to be on readability.

Point size and leading is expressed as 10/12 or 21/21.5 plus the alignment. This is pronounced ten on twelve or twenty-one on twenty-one and a half. In these cases, 10 and 21 are the point size and 12 and 21.5 are the leading in points. So, a common statement would be something like this: body copy is normally 10/12 justified left. This would be a paragraph with 10-point type and 12-point leading set justified with the last line flush left—like this paragraph and all the body copy in this book. When the point size and leading are the same, as in 16/16, it is referred to as being set solid. If the leading is less than the point size it is negative leading.

Leading is determined by font design, point size, line length, and reading distance. All fonts have differing built-in line spacing.

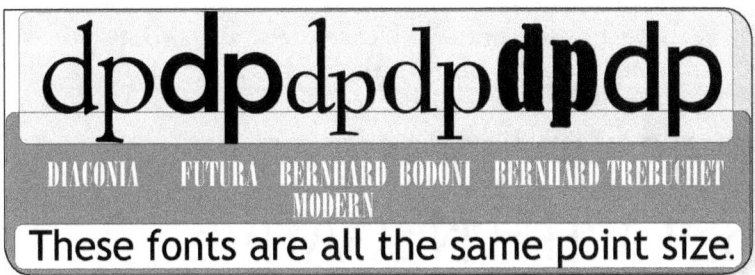

As you can see above, Futura has none and Bernhard Modern had a lot. Bernhard has the most built-in leading. Bernhard Modern also has a very small x-height. As a result, if we accept that normal body copy is 10/12 (and it is), then Futura should probably be set at 10/13 and Bernhard Modern at 14/13 (or more, even up to 16/15 or so).

Some leading norms for normal reading distance:

- Tiny type: Type smaller than 7 point is usually set solid. With type set that small, you usually don't want people reading it. It is used for the small type used to produce legalese [which no one reads anyway].

- Body copy: This is the normal reading copy in your documents. It is rigidly required to be 10/12 by traditional publishers, as mentioned. However, when you have the control, those figures should be adjusted by x-height and built-in line spacing. Larger x-heights require smaller point sizes. A large amount of built-in spacing between the top of the ascenders and the bottoms of the descenders in the line above takes less leading. Long line lengths require more leading. In general, bold, sans serif, or condensed fonts need more leading.

- Headers: Headlines and subheads are commonly set solid. The larger the point size used, the less leading is needed.

🌶 **All caps:** Setting type in all caps often requires negative leading. This means that the leading is less than the point size. If you think about it, the reasoning should be clear. All caps have no descenders. Descenders are about a third of the point size. So headlines in all caps might well be set 36/28 or so.

THIS HEADLINE IS SET WITH NEGATIVE LEADING OF 30/27

4. Tabs and fixed spaces

Spaces cause many other problems for people trained in typewriting. On a typewriter, the spacebar is a known quantity. This is because every character in monospaced type is the same width—even the space. This is definitely not true for type. In fact, in type, the space band is often a different size than it was the last time you hit the key.

This is caused by several factors. First, the word space character in various fonts varies in width. There is no standard. This space also changes with point size, of course. This is not a problem with typewriters because they only have one size and one font. Because of typewriter-based training, people accustomed to word processors do most of their horizontal spacing with multiple spaces. This is one reason why the first thing you usually have to do with word processor copy is eliminate the double spaces.

More than this, word spacing is one of the defaults that should be set to your standards. Page layout programs give you very precise control over word spacing [word processors have none]. Finally, word spacing varies with every line when setting justified copy.

Justification

When you are setting a line of justified type, you determine a justification zone. When the last word that fits in a line ends in this justification zone, any remaining space in the column width is evenly divided and added to the word spaces in the line. If the last word does not reach the zone, the length of the zone is divided and added to the spaces in the line (any additional space is divided and added as letterspacing between every letter in the line).

What this means is that the spaces on every line are a different width in justified copy. Look at the gray boxes on the first and third line above. InDesign works hard to minimize this on a paragraph basis, justifying the whole paragraph at a time. More than that, the word spaces are different from paragraph to paragraph whenever size, font, or defaults change. As a result, you never really know how wide a spacebar character will be.

Here are several sample rows of type to demonstrate how justification works in your paragraphs.

Leftover space at the end of a line is divided by the number of spaces and added to each space. Fixed spaces are not adjusted by this.

Here are several sample rows of type to demonstrate how justification works in your paragraphs.

The problem of predictable spaces has been solved by using some more letterpress solutions. When type was composed, it was brought out to a rectangle no matter what the alignment was—right, left, centered, or justified. The characters used to do this were blank slugs, called quads, that were a little lower than type-height so they would not print accidentally. These quads came in three widths: em, en, and el, plus what were called hair spaces. The el space is long gone; it is now usually called a thin space. InDesign has all four types. Word has ems and ens [you can add a command in your Insert menu]. The recent versions of InDesign have added several more that typographers deem essential. You don't really need them except for very difficult composition— like covers and such.

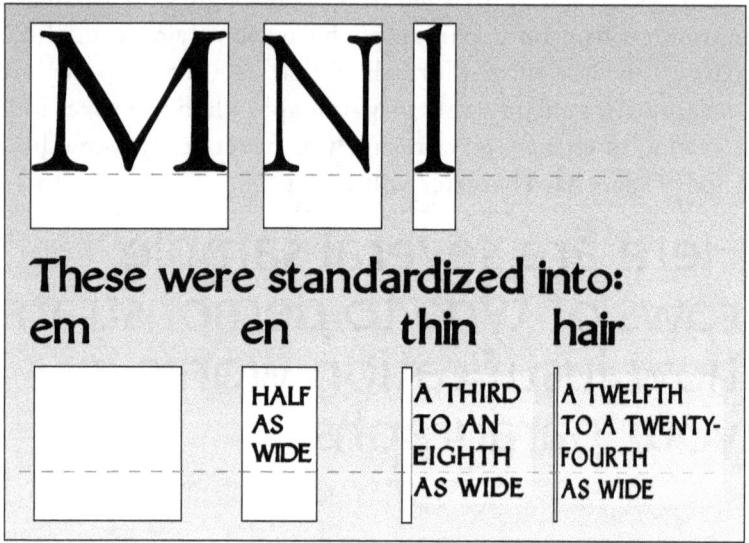

Originally these characters were blanks the width of an *m*, *n*, and *l*, respectively. Of course, they were standardized. These spaces are now defined as follows: an em space is the square of the point size; an en space is the same height, of course, but half as wide; and a thin space varies. InDesign's hair space is one-twenty-fourth of an em.

These fixed spaces are used a lot. For example, they should always be used for custom hand-spacing, because the spacebar can vary proportionally if you change the point size. Fixed spaces remain proportionally consistent. Another fact to bear in mind is that lining numbers are normally an en space wide. This means that an en should be used as a blank when lining up numbers (an em for two numbers) for accountants and bookkeepers.

Tabular construction

Custom spacing should normally be done with tabs. Typesetting tabs are much more powerful than typewriting tabs. They come in four kinds: left, right, centered, and decimal. Actually these decimal tabs can be aligned on any character you choose like the x in 2x4. All tabs can be set up with leaders. These leaders can be lines, dotted lines, or any repeating character you need. Again this has been extended radically so that you can now make leaders out of a repeating set of up to 8 characters. You're only limited by your imagination. [Of course, tabs do not work at all in ePubs or Kindle—you'll probably need a table.]

Word processor tab use

One of the additional problems you will have with word processing copy is poor tab use. A single tab is often used for the first-line indent. You will have to delete that and set up a first line indent. Because many word processor users do not know how to set tabs, they just use the default tabs that come every half inch. As a result, you will often find several tabs in a row—used like multiple spaces. They will all have to be changed to a single tab. In addition, because most do not know how to do bulleted or numbered lists, every line is commonly returned manually using multiple tabs. I'm certainly glad you never do anything like that. You will have to get rid of all of them. You will get very fast with Find & Change.

In general, get used to the idea that the spacebar should only be hit once. It cannot be used to line up portions of different lines. They will constantly be out of alignment. In fact, you need to be a little careful. On a computer keyboard, any key that is held down will automatically repeat, including the spacebar. In typesetting there is no legitimate use of the double space. The same is almost true of the tab, but there are exceptions with tabs.

5. En and em dashes

The next major change we need to discuss is dashes. Typewriters only have one—the hyphen. Type has three—the hyphen, the en dash, and the em dash. All three have very specific usage rules.

HYPHEN   EN DASH   EM DASH

Hyphen: This is the character used to hyphenate words at the end of a line and to create compound words. For example, 10-point is the normal point size for book publishers' body copy. In fact, hyphenation is used no other place. So, you have a couple keystrokes to learn.

En dash: This dash is an en long. It is used with numbers, spans, or ranges. For example, pages 24–39 or 6:00–9:00 or May 7–12. It is a typo to use a hyphen in these cases. The keystroke for an en-dash is Option+Hyphen.

 A special case: In rare cases, hyphens and en dashes need to be mixed for clarity. I used one a few paragraphs back when presenting the width of a hair space for InDesign. It seemed to me to be easier to read and understand one–twenty-fourth of an em with the en dash between the one and twenty-fourth. This is the typographer's decision to make.

Em dash: This dash is an em long. It is a punctuation mark. The keystroke for an em-dash is Option+Shift+Hyphen. Grammatically it is stronger than a comma but weaker than a period. Other than that, there is no standard anymore.

American English is a living language in constant flux. These changes have accelerated in recent years. In many cases, there are no rules anymore. Em dashes are used more every year. In many ways they are very helpful—but traditionalists tend to have bad reactions. Typewriters use a double hyphen for the em dash. This is an embarrassing error to professionals. In fact, it is one of the sure signs of amateurism. It must be fixed.

Finally, do not think you will not be caught. Hyphens are about a thin space wide. They are higher above the baseline than en or em dashes. Also, they are commonly slanted up with little swashes on the ends (although you see swashes for all three in Contenu).

Dashes on a PC, in Word

After disabling the AutoCorrect option, you'll have to enter an em dash manually. Fortunately, there are three easy methods.

En dash:

- Press [Ctrl]+-. You must use the minus sign on the numeric keypad.

- Hold down the [Alt] key and type 0150 on the numeric keypad.

- Choose Symbol from the Insert menu, click the Special Characters tab, highlight the en dash, and click Insert.

Em dash:

- Press [Ctrl]+[Alt]+-. You must use the minus sign on the numeric keypad; if you use the hyphen character on the alphanumeric keypad, Word will change the cursor.

- Hold down the [Alt] key and type 0151 on the numeric keypad.

- Choose Symbol from the Insert menu, click the Special Characters tab, highlight the em dash, and click Insert.

6. Real quotes and apostrophes

Here is another place where typewriters are limited by the lack of characters. All typewriters have is inch and foot marks. Quotation marks and apostrophes look very different. This is another typographical embarrassment when used incorrectly. There are more keystrokes you need to learn, though you can solve most of the problems by turning on Use Typographer's Quotes in Type page of Preferences. The shortcut is an on/off toggle command:
Command+Option+Shift+' by default.

Feet' Inches" Quotes "double" & 'single'

Again it is important to use the right characters. An apostrophe is a single close quote.

Dumb quotes

The typewriter inch/foot marks in almost all fonts are actually wrong. They are the mathematical marks used for prime and double-prime. True inch and foot marks are slanted a couple of degrees. Some typographers italicize the prime and double prime glyphs. Typographers often call prime and double-prime marks dumb quotes from their use by typists.

Language differences

One of the more disconcerting things to keep track of in this increasingly global society is usage differences in the languages. For example, in America, we are taught to use double quotes for a quote and single quotes for quotes within a quote. British usage is the opposite.

Other languages use completely different characters or changes like open double quotes which look like close double quotes on the baseline—to our American eyes.

Increasingly, we are designing documents set in multiple languages. It is important to keep track of these things. Consider, for instance, the Spanish practice for questions, ¿Que pasa? or expletives, ¡Vámonos!

Guillemots: ‹ › « »

Single and double guillemots are used by several European languages in place of curly quotes. For French and Italian, they point out like «thus». In German they often point in, according to Bringhurst, using »this style«. But then I am not a linguist so I don't know the ins and outs. The point is to be careful.

Bringhurst's work, *The Elements of Typographic Style*, has a great deal of information on specific typographic usage in other languages for those of you doing a lot of this work. It is important to do it right so the reader is not offended.

7. No underlines

The next difference has to do with the physical nature of typewriters. Because they only have one size of type, there is no way to emphasize words except for all caps and underlining. Underlining is necessary for these antiques. In typesetting, underlining ruins the carefully crafted descenders. In addition, the underlines that come with the type are usually too heavy and poorly placed. They also compromise readability and type color by messing with the white space between lines.

If you decide that an underline is an appropriate solution, please adjust the color and location with your Underline Options dialog to avoid compromising the readability of the type.

The goal of typesetting is to make clean, elegant type that is read without distraction. Underlining is almost as bad as outlines and shadows, as far as professionals are concerned. They ruin the unique characteristics of the font. At times they serve a useful design function, but this kind of modification should be used very discreetly.

How to deal with underlines typographically—change them

When receiving copy typed by others, you will usually find body copy littered with underlines. Our job, as typesetters, is to convert those underlines to the proper usage. **Proper Names** should be set in a bold version of the font. Periodic names like *National Geographic* or *People* magazines must be in italics. Words that are simple *emphasis* should also be set in italic. *For strong emphasis*, you may want to change fonts.

8. No ALL CAPS

As mentioned in the underline section, setting letters in all caps is the other way to emphasize words on a typewriter. Typesetting has many more options. There are many more options like *italic*, **bold**, ***bold italic***, small caps. Plus we can use a larger size, and more. **In fact, we can simply change the font used.**

28: How Can I Make It Better?

There is something else, however. Studies have shown that type in all caps is around 40 percent less legible than caps and lowercase, or just lowercase. All caps is also much longer than the same word set C&lc.

Because our major purpose is to get the reader to read our piece and act on the message, you should never use all caps (unless you have a good reason). For example, all caps is often used to make a piece of type less legible and therefore to de-emphasize it. Some people say that all-cap headlines are fine, but I would disagree unless you are careful.

Readability

Readability is an interesting and complicated phenomenon. Everyone has theories. What most agree on is that people recognize letters by the distinctive outlines on the top of the letter shapes.

This is the major reason why setting type in all caps is so counter-productive. Because uppercase letters tend to be in rectangular boxes the tops of characters tend to look very similar.

ΛTTD ΛCTIVE WOMΛN
is not nearly as easy to decipher as
cowardly lion
and the bottom halves almost never work,

ılıtcllcctual ɔllov
as in(intellectual snob)

As you can see, the straight line formed by the tops of the caps and the bottoms of the lowercase (even the descenders do not help) are not distinct enough to recognize easily. Please, remember that difficulty is not a good attribute of reading material. These readability issues are primary to typesetting. You really need to keep track. You can read it because you set it. Your readers do not have that benefit.

9. Letterspacing, kerning, and tracking

Here is another typesetting capability that cannot even be considered by word processors. We mentioned letterspacing earlier. Letterspacing is the built-in spacing between characters in a font. The basic idea is that the white space between letters should be identical for all letter pairs. Obviously, this is not simple or easy. AT, OOPS, and silly have very different spacing problems—especially the ill. The better the font, the better the letterspacing. In very cheap fonts, individual letters may be far to the left or right. I bought one once where the lowercase *r* was always at least 9 points to the left.

Awkwardly is a very difficult word to space well. In the examples below, I have used vertical white lines to indicate the edges of the glyphs. The rectangles show overlap.

Normal: the edges of the characters touch each other

Awkwardly

Tracking: all letters are moved an equal amount

Awkwardly

If I track until the Aw looks good, the rest of the spacing is trashed.

Kerning: All letter pairs are adjusted separately

Awkwardly

The Aw kerning is the same as the tracking, but all the rest of the glyphs are kerned individually. The kw is still a problem. If I was really using this word large, I would space it wider [for the dly].

Tracking

Tracking is the official term used to replace letterspacing in digital typesetting now that we can move letters either closer together or farther apart. In reality, either term can be used and understood. The actual procedure for tracking simply inserts or removes an equal amount of space around every letter selected or affected.

Although tracking is used all the time by typographic novices, it is despicable to traditional professionals. Quality typefaces have the letterspacing carefully designed into the font. Changing the tracking for stylistic reasons or fashion changes the color of the type at the very least. A paragraph tracked tighter looks darker. At worst, it can make the type color of the page look splotchy.

Tracking suffers from the vagaries of fashion. In the 1980s, it was very common to see extremely tight tracking in everything. Tight tracking severely compromises readability by obscuring lettershapes.

Global tracking changes: If you are using a display font for your body copy, it will commonly be set too tight. In this case you may want to increase the tracking, globally, for the entire document. The same is true when using a text font for heads. Here you want to move the letters closer.

Kerning

Kerning is a different thing altogether. Here we step outside of word processing. Here the problem is with letter pairs. Word cannot adjust the space between individual pairs of letters. There are thousands of different letter pairs. I guess the total would be around 20,000 or 40,000 pairs. There is no way to set up the spacing around letters to cover all situations: AR is a very different situation than AV; To than Th; AT than AW.

Literally thousands of different kerned pairs are needed to make a perfectly kerned font. Some kern together and some kern apart. Most of them can only be seen at the larger point sizes. Here again we see the difference between excellent and cheap fonts. Professional fonts have around 1,000 kerning pairs built into the font metrics. Cheap fonts commonly have a couple dozen or none at all. Quality fonts have kerning designed into about a thousand letter pairs.

In addition, all professional publishing programs allow you to adjust kerning for individual pairs. InDesign gives you keyboard shortcuts (most often Option+Left Arrow and

Option+Right Arrow). Adding the Command key multiples the amount moved.

InDesign offers Optical kerning which automatically checks the letterspacing and adjusts it for you. It does a remarkable job. In Word, in the Font dialog box, under character spacing, you can turn on Kerning for the font. But it merely uses the kerning built into the font.

 We are always expected to check the kerning on all type larger than about 18-point: Yes, you really are required to hand kern all headlines if necessary. It's the only way, in most cases. Unkerned type looks cheap and unprofessional.

10. Be careful with hyphens.

Because typeset line endings are automatic, so is the hyphenation. You can turn it on or off. Hyphenation is done by dictionary. You can set up the hyphens when you add new words to the user dictionary (see help).

Another problem is that automatic hyphenation can create hyphens for many consecutive lines. Here there is sharp debate. Most of us agree that two hyphens in a row should be the maximum (a three-hyphen "stack" looks odd). Page layout software allows you to set that limit. Many set the limit at one.

Yet another problem comes when you run into something like two hyphens in a row; then a normal line; then two more hyphens. The final problem comes when the program hyphenates part of a compound word. **Be careful with hyphens!**

Finally, never hyphenate a word in a headline or subhead. It just isn't done. In fact, almost all headers should be carefully examined if they go to two lines or more. Normally they need to be broken for sense with soft-returns [Shift+Return]. In your header paragraph styles, simply turn hyphenation off. I originally turned hyphenation off for this entire book. I later turned it back on for the body copy—simply because the type color was no longer smooth.

11. Eliminate widows and orphans

As Roger Black states in his pioneering work, *Desktop Design Power* (Random House, 1990, out of print) "Widows are the surest sign of sloppy typesetting." The problems arise as soon as we start trying to simply define the words. See the subsection below on orphans.

I am using the most common definitions (also the ones used by Black). A widow is a short line at the end of a paragraph that is much too short. What is too short? Again, there is sharp debate. The best answer is that the last line must have at least two complete words and those two words must be at least eight characters total. Bringhurst says at least four characters. (But then his typography is filled with short sentence fragments at the end of paragraphs that look horrible, as far as I am concerned.) You need to eliminate all of them like the word "above" which follows: a-bove.

Orphans (paragraph fragments in columns)

The software will really mess you up here, if you are not careful. Programmers usually have no idea what a widow is. Often they confuse widows with orphans. InDesign uses Bringhurst's definitions. I do not know any traditional typesetter who uses these conventions, but then I only know a few hundred or so. I agree with people like Sandee Cohen, Roger Black, Robin Williams, and many others. Actually, everyone agrees what excellent type should look like. There are only semantic differences—word definitions.

An orphan is a short paragraph or paragraph fragment left by itself at the top or bottom of a column. In Bringhurst-speak (and he is marvelously witty), a widow is an orphan at the bottom of a column. An orphan is one left at the top of a column. A classic example is a subhead left at the bottom of one column with the body copy starting at the top of the next column.

InDesign allows you to control both of these problems fairly well with their *keeps controls*. A keeps control, in the option menu of the paragraph dialog or panel, allows you to determine if a paragraph must stay with the following paragraph (in the case of the subhead, for example). It also allows you to set the minimum paragraph fragment allowed at either end of a paragraph. This is normally a two-line minimum, top or bottom, beginning or end. Be careful—all existing software considers a widow to be an orphan at the bottom of a column and an orphan comes only at the top (they are both orphans).

Fixing widows (last lines of paragraphs)

Bad paragraph widows mess up the type color. They allow a blank white area to appear between paragraphs which stands out like a sore thumb. There is no way to eliminate them except by hand. The best way is editorially. In other words, rewrite the paragraph! Occasionally that is not possible. In that case, you must carefully adjust the hyphenation, horizontal scale, point size, or word spacing (in that order).

Here we get into local formatting. However, a difficult widow can often be eliminated no other way.

- Hyphenation: Often you can eliminate a widow by simply adding a hyphenation point to a word with a discretionary hyphen. A discretionary hyphen is a character that places a breaking point in a word that is invisible unless a hyphen is needed. The shortcut varies. The InDesign default is Command+Shift+Hyphen. Sadly, this character is often not available on the PC.

- Horizontal scale: Here we get into another of those typographic purist fracases. Using horizontal scaling to condense or expand letterforms makes these guys and gals freak. However, plus or minus 5% is invisible. This is the easiest way to pull back a widow. Even most typographers can't see the changes.

- Point size: Make the point size a half-point smaller. As you recall, a point is about the smallest difference the human eye can see. An entire paragraph with type that is a half-point smaller is an invisible change.

Word spacing: In justified copy, the word space is elastic. You'll need to customize this setting because the defaults are terrible. Let's say your software is set at 80% minimum, 100% normal, and 115% maximum. If you change the normal to 95%, you move the words a little closer and might eliminate a widow. [I talk about this option more in Appendix B]

 You must be gentle or your corrections will stand out worse than the widow: The point size should never be changed more than a half point, for example. Always make your changes to the entire paragraph. Extremely short paragraphs often cannot be fixed, except to "break for sense." This means placing soft returns so that each short line makes sense by itself (as much as possible). Remember, the best method is rewriting the paragraph to add or subtract a word or two to get rid of the widow.

The absolute worst orphan is a widow at the top of a new page—especially if it is the hyphenated back half of the last word. Other horrible typos are: widow at the top of a column; subhead at the bottom, as mentioned; a kicker separated from its headline; and a subhead with one line of body copy at the bottom of a column.

These errors must be eliminated at the proofing stage. This is what we mean by massaging a document into shape. Corrections like these are among the primary factors that cause people to react to a design. If they are missing, your design will be classed with amateur productions like school and bureaucrat output.

12. Use bulleted lists.

The use of bullets and dingbats is unknown to typists. Bulleted lists are an extremely effective means of attracting the reader's attention. In fact, there has been a lot of study to find out what readers see and respond to. These are the paragraphs you use to attract the reader's eye or to re-attract it if it is wandering in boredom. The readership order goes like this:

- First, **picture captions**—everyone looks at the pictures first: Photos are checked out before drawings, unless the illustrations are exceptional. The caption should be the synopsis of the major benefit in the story to the reader.

- Second, **headlines**—primarily because of size and placement: The headline should also be the synopsis of the major benefit in the story to the reader. No reader reads everything. You need to tell them why this story is important to them.

- Third, **callouts or pull quotes**—these are quotes pulled from the copy or statements about the copy: that are enlarged to the point where they become interesting graphics in their own right. They are exceptionally valuable in pages of nothing but body copy to capture the wandering eye. Care must be taken. An improperly pulled quote can change the editorial focus of the article.

- Fourth, **bulleted or numbered lists**—like this one: Bulleted lists are read by scanning readers before subheads, drop caps, or any of the other graphic leads commonly used. The assumption is that lists are synopses of the surrounding copy. Readers use them to determine if the rest of the story is worth reading.

Dingbats

Dingbats

There are hundreds of dingbat fonts. Many of them are excellent sources of fashionable clip art. Here are a few samples from three fonts called MiniPics -Confetti, MiniPics -LilDinos, & MiniPics -LilFaces.

With typesetting we have even more options than simple bullets. Dingbats are fonts made up of graphics. Every keystroke is a different graphic. Zapf Dingbats is a font that almost everyone has on a Mac. The ones to the left are from Wingdings, which has a similar function on a PC. Almost everyone has several dingbat fonts, even if they don't know it.

Font creation programs allow you to use a logo in a font. Top-quality dingbat fonts are a good way to pick up a collection of clip art that can be used as you type. For a time, dingbat fonts became one of the best sources of fashionable art. Using dingbats for bullets increases the attraction of the list. Just be careful that the reader is led to read the copy and not simply be amused by your graphic.

 Often dingbats are graphic enough to make excellent starts and/or pieces of logo design: You may want to buy several of these font resources. MyFonts.com has a huge collection of dingbat fonts. Several type designers specialize in dingbat font design.

13. Use small caps.

Small caps are a specialized letterform as we've mentioned. Page layout software creates small caps by proportionally shrinking capital letters. This makes them appear to be too light. The best method is to use fonts that have custom-designed small caps. There were few font families like this prior to this millennium. But now, many of the OpenType font families have real small caps. The problem, of course, is that ePubs and Kindle books do not support true small caps.

There are only a few places where small caps are required. However, I strongly agree with Bringhurst here. He has many other places where he recommends small caps. What we are basically saying is that strings of caps within body copy should be SMALL CAPS. Otherwise these acronyms and abbreviations appear to be shouting.

There are several things attached to this position. First of all, this use of small caps is coupled with the use of old style numbers (or if you use my fonts, small cap figures). Second, small caps are often, but not necessarily, used only in body copy. Your task, should you accept this venture, will be to convince your copy editor that this is correct procedure. Most of them are using old, newspaper-based, manuals of style. Basing typographic style on newspapers is like basing fashionable dress on Wally World.

Nevertheless, there are a few places where you use small caps even if you do not have true small caps. For times and dates, the proper use is not A.M. or AM or a.m. but AM. The same is true of PM, AD, BC, BCE, and CE. In these cases, you should always use small caps with no periods. But then that is just my opinion. But what about statements like USA 1776? Here the determining factor is whether or not you have oldstyle or small cap numbers in your font. In general, you should always use oldstyle numbers in body copy, at least. So, all strings of caps like this should be small caps: ASCII, USA, UN, USSR, CIA, NASCAR, and so on.

Adding letter space for readability

To increase readability, you will need to add letter space to the small cap strings (though a good font will have this built in). This should be designed into the font you use. You should also do this if you are using all caps for headlines. Seriously, any time you are using words made up of capital letters you need to add space between the letters until they become readable. The guiding principle is to add as much as you can without causing the letters to separate into individual characters instead of a unified word.

Lining numbers with all caps

Even though we have stated that lining numbers are really only appropriate for bookkeepers, accountants, and CPAS, there are other appropriate uses. One of these is in the midst of all caps.

GOD BLESS AMERICA! REMEMBER 9/11/2001 & 2008.

Yes, there are occasions you will be using all caps. You will have to letterspace to help readability. In this situation oldstyle numbers would look foolish.

Readability is crucial;
common sense is required.

14. First-line indents

We have briefly touched on first-line indents for body copy paragraphs. This is the preferred method of telling the reader that a new topic sentence is being developed—a new thought expressed. I also mentioned my practice of adding a point or two after paragraphs to help the reader see that first-line indent on a busy page.

The amount of that first-line indent is up to you. You're the designer. The norm is somewhere between a quarter inch and a half inch. Robert says that the minimum is an en, but that is far below what I would call a minimum. An en just tends to look like a mistake. Some say the indent should equal the lead so when using 10/12 you should indent 12 points. Many specify an em, which in the 10/12 example would be 10 points. That is barely over an eighth of an inch—too small for me.

The first-line indent should equal the left indent of your lists.

Actually, I think the first line indent is more intertwined than any of those intellectually fine sounding indents of fixed spaces. One of the things to consider as you set up your paragraph styles and page layout is that second consistent interior line which is made by your first-line indents, the left indent of your lists, the left indent of your body heads, and the left indent of your quotes.

As a result, I have personally arrived at a first-line indent of .4 inch. You may want to use less or more, but IMHO anything less than a quarter inch (18 points) just looks like a mistake. It is not really visible; so it merely irritates. Anything more than a half inch makes the eye feel like it has to lunge in to find the beginning.

15. Drop caps

One of the typographic devices used to indicate the beginning of a story or chapter is the drop cap. In this use, the first letter or letters of the first paragraph is (are) made large enough to be three, four, or five lines of type tall and inset into the paragraph.

LOVE is patient; love is kind; love is not envious or boastful or arrogant or rude. It does not insist on its own way; it is not irritable or resentful; it does not rejoice in wrongdoing, but rejoices in the truth.

Love bears all things, believes all things, hopes all things, endures all things.

The first-lines of that paragraph are tabbed around the letter or letters. First of all, this is very easy with page layout software. InDesign's implementation allows you to drop as many letters as you want as far as you want—interactively. You can just click the buttons in the Paragraph or Control panel until you like what you see.

Often, the drop cap is in a radically different font. It can be set very dramatically in a flowing script that hangs off in the left margin. It is often in a different color. Commonly used are the illuminated capitals of the medieval scribes.

Mainly, it needs to be dramatic.

The largest mistake with drop caps is overuse. They need to be used very sparingly. As you can see in the four paragraphs above, multiple drop caps are merely confusing. They should never be used more than once on a page. Really, they should only be used once—for the first paragraph of a story, article, or chapter.

16. Proper accents for languages

When you are using a word or phrase from another language, always accent it properly. Some of these things are commonly missed. Words like résumé, moiré, façade, and the like have entered common usage in English. But if you are using the pine nuts from the Southwest in your cooking, they are piñon nuts. Being from New Mexico, I know the ubiquitous and unique New Mexican hot peppers are chilé.

40: How Can I Make It Better?

Chili is that weird stuff (to my taste inedible) with beans and/or meat from Texas.

This type of typography is only common courtesy. You need to be aware that in the old Commonwealth it is still cheque and lorry. In those countries, corporations get plural verbs—as in: Shell Oil are drilling five new off-shore wells south of Norway.

In America, you need to be very careful of local usage. I mentioned the chilé example already. In speech, what is sillier (or more annoying) than an outsider calling the fertile valley south of Portland the Will•i-a•mette' Valley instead of the Will•**am'**•et as it is locally pronounced? You will find that all locales have local usage. You need to use it.

We have just gotten started.

I could go on for many pages with typographic niceties. This is just a first introduction to type. The Chinese showed their wisdom again by considering calligraphy to be the highest form of art.

Once you understand type, you will see its beauty. Well-drawn type is absolutely gorgeous. After a while, you begin to understand why some of the best graphic designs are simply type.

This goes far beyond simple beauty, though. Excellent type is much easier to read. It eases customer fears. It helps make good experiences (think about a dinner menu at a fine restaurant coupled with a marriage proposal). It is what makes your book a joy to read (assuming you can write ;-).

Setting up your Word or word processing document

First of all, you need to realize that everything needs to be formatted with paragraph styles. The basic body copy style in Word is Normal. What you need to do is Modify Normal and make it fit your needs for your book. You should do this for your ebooks as well—even though we are discussing books for print in this little booklet.

However, we are setting things up so the conversion to ePUB is as painless as possible. So, we need to deal with the realities of HTML. The basic issue with HTML is that there are only 7-9 styles available for use. Let's look at them a bit:

- p: body copy. This is what is called Normal in Word.
- h1: Headline. Word calls this Heading 1.
- h2: Subhead. Word calls this Heading 2.
- h3: Subhead2. Word calls this Heading 3.
- h4: Subhead3. Word calls this Heading 4.
- h5: Subhead4. Word calls this Heading 5.
- h6: Subhead5. Word calls this Heading 6.
- ol: Ordered List. Numbered list.
- ul: Unordered list. Bulleted list.

So, what do we do with all the other paragraph styles we need? Now you have come to the crux of the problem. I will not get into that here. Suffice it to say that quotes can be set as Heading 5 with suitable font, size, and indent adjustments. The same is true of Caption, which can be done with Heading 6—modified into usefulness.

Lists

Here we have a major problem with ebooks as they do not do lists well at all. Just format each type of list you use with a List style. That is the best you can hope for. If you get the Word document into a professional page layout application like InDesign, the best option at this time is to convert the list into text. But those options are still very limited. The result is that print lists will look very different and much better than ebook lists [except for PDFs, of course].

The main thing is consistency

I just produced the book versions for a new author. She had a byline under a quote beginning each chapter. Originally, all the paragraphs were just locally formatted versions of Normal. I got around that by hand-formatting each paragraph. But that was just the beginning.

In front of the quote I found:

- Space, double-hyphen, space
- Double-hyphen, space
- Hyphen, space
- Space, hyphen, space
- Hyphen
- Space, hyphen, space, hyphen
- Em dash
- Em dash, space
- Space, em dash, space.

It took me over a half hour to simply get that consistent throughout the 20 chapters [em dash-thin space]. There was no way to fix it with a simple Find & Change. I had the same problem with the quotes. Some had manual returns after every line, some every other line, and some just at the end of the quote. They also had to be fixed manually, instance by instance. If you simply do these things consistently you'll save the formatter a lot of time and hassle.

Some body copy paragraphs used a tab for the first line indent. Some used 5 spaces. Some had none. Now, I wasn't upset or surprised. That is why my quote was where it was in cost. But, hopefully you can see the problem. If you do not use a designer, you'll drive yourself nuts.

The main thing that makes a book "look like a book" is the formatting, the page layout and the text styles used. It is very important that you make a plan and use it.

Normal word processing issues

Yes, I know that this is very basic, known material for experienced book designers. When a book designer is using a word processing file for the raw copy, it is often necessary to spend many minutes (if not hours) removing all the bad formatting before that copy can be flowed into a page layout with any degree of freedom.

However, for new authors these issues are unheard of. As standard as they are for typography, few people have typographic knowledge or training. Just reading the first part of this book, with some of the basics of typography, has probably shown you several things you know you are doing wrong. However, simply making these mistakes consistently will enable your formatter [or yourself] to clean them up quickly and efficiently.

For a manuscript from a newbie author,
the list of problems goes on for quite a while:

- **Double spaces:** All the multiple spaces have to be deleted.
- **Copy typed in all caps:** This normally must be converted to C&lc. I suggest setting up those shortcuts for case in applications like InDesign where it is possible.
- Using a tab for the first line indent
- **Centering headlines with multiple spaces:** there are many places where many spaces can be added
- Multiple returns
- Using multiple tabs: this is usually done instead of using hard or soft returns to go to the next line or next paragraph in a bulleted list

- Bad lists: Lining up each line in a bulleted list with a hard return at the end of the line then multiple spaces or tabs in front of the next line in the paragraph
- Extra Space characters: at the beginning and end of paragraphs

Placed Word documents often have many strange character substitutions

You may find things like an Ö instead of " and Ó instead of " and many more. Often the Upper ASCII characters on a PC get scrambled when added to a Mac document.

There are others; but these will usually get you where you need to go. There is a complete pop-up list in Find/Change in InDesign. You might learn many of them if you are working in a fast production environment with a large quantity of different clients (like an art department in a printing company).

Dealing with word processor copy from others

Sooner or later, it is likely that you will be using copy typed and or written by someone else. For the moment I will assume that it is in a format you can read and import. Often though (unless all of your copy comes from in-house), the copy will have been input by an author or typist with no training in printing requirements. It will be filled with multiple spaces and returns. Copy that should be italic will be underlined, or at the very least have quotes around it. The tabs will be made with multiple spaces. Centering will be done with the space bar. The list is almost endless.

You will have to eliminate all of these typos before you can format your copy. You will have to use a special code in the Find/Change dialog box to search for and replace many of the invisible characters. You can do much more with GREP—but that is far too much coding for me. InDesign uses a popup menu at the end of both the Find field and the Change field to add the special characters you need to replace with the special characters you need to add. Sometimes it works to simply copy the error and paste it into the Find field. The list that follows is just an aid in memorization if you are working in InDesign.

- ^p is code to find or replace a hard return
- ^n is code to find or replace a soft return
- ^t is code to find or replace a tab

Here is a procedure that will eliminate most common word processor typos in a few brief steps:

1. **Multiple spaces:** Use the Find/Change command to change all double spaces to single spaces. Just type in the space key twice in the Find field and once in the Change To field. Then click change all.

2. **Multiple returns:** Use Find/Change command to change all double returns to single returns. **[^p^p to ^p]**. Then click change all.

In most cases you will also have to do the following steps to clean up your paragraph structure

3. **Multiple tabs:** Use Find/Change to eliminate all multiple tabs. In almost all cases these are used because typists usually do not set up tabs, they use the default half inch tabs and just use multiple tabs to clear things over far enough for their design comfort. **[^t^t to ^t]**. Then click change all

4. **Eliminate spaces at the beginning and end of paragraphs:** These are remnants of the multiple space, tab and return in steps 1–3 above. Use **[^pSpace to ^p]** for spaces at the beginning & **[Space^p to ^p]** for space at the end. Then click change all

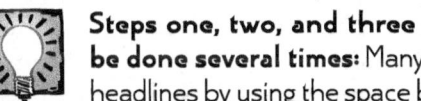

Steps one, two, and three may have to be done several times: Many typists center headlines by using the space bar. This could use ten to thirty spaces. Each time you run the command, you will halve the number of spaces until there is only one left. The same is true of returns. Often spacing, or moving to the next page, is accomplished by adding many extra spaces or many extra returns. The same is true of tabs where complicated tabular materials are put together with the default half-inch tabs repeated as necessary to get things to line up.

When you have the copy cleaned up, it is often necessary to eliminate all foreign formatting. Occasionally it is quicker to simply open the imported styles (they will have a small icon [a tiny floppy disc] at the end of the style instead of a shortcut) one by one and change the formatting within the imported style. However, this is usually false economy because all the based-on and next-style settings will be messed up (at the very least).

 Before you eliminate the formatting, make sure you print out hard copy: so you do not lose the location of bold, italic, and underlined copy. You will need to fix all of these things and eliminating all bad formatting will eliminate these errors as well—making them difficult to find or impossible, forcing you to start over.

5. Wipe out formatting: Select all to select the entire story. Then format everything to [Basic Paragraph]. If you are working in Word, choose Clear Formatting.

6. Clear Overrides: With everything still selected, click on the Clear Overrides button in the Paragraph Control Panel. You can try holding down the Command+Shift keys as you click on the [Basic Paragraph] style–but this often does not get all the overrides.

7. Format everything to your basic body copy style: With everything still selected, format everything to body copy. This is why the style is called body copy, because the vast majority of the copy is set in this style. Doing this will enable faster reformatting because all that will have changed are the heads, subheads, and special

paragraphs. Plus it will make your text as small as it will ever be to give you a better idea of how many pages you are going to need.

This erases all foreign formatting

These procedures will eliminate all the foreign formatting (which is almost certainly littered with typestyles and fonts not found on your machine). In addition, the formatting that was used probably contrasts greatly with your layout. Word processors never format in multiple columns effectively, for one small example—nor do they have sidebars.

Now you are ready to format everything with your style palette. Edit your styles by eliminating all the imported styles from the palette. Often the fastest procedure is to eliminate all styles and then copy styles from a template you have set up properly.

Although this process may seem like a real hassle, it is much faster than anything else. Ideally, your copy will come in properly formatted. In reality, this rarely happens except with books you write yourself or regular clients you have helped before. Even then you often have to train them.

A general guideline is this: If the copy was not keyed in by a trained typesetting professional, all formatting probably should be eliminated before you go to work—simply to save you time.

 **Another thing that helps is to spell check in your word processor and in InDesign:** All spell checkers are a little different. Some catch initial caps on sentences, some catch double words, some catch transposed letters, some check proper names. All have a different set of features. So, the operative principle is spell check in your word processor, and then spell check again in InDesign after everything is formatted.

Obviously, this is just an introduction to the entire area of self-publishing professionally. Once you hae a completed manuscript, then the production work of book design really begins. But that's another book.

Other books & resources

I have a similar book to this for people looking for guidance about marketing the books they've published. I don't have much help for normal people as my focus is on deeply committed Christian authors. But if you are one of those, you will find this helpful:

A Christian Self-Publishing Guide to Sell Books & eBooks Online

This book discusses the unique issues facing committed Christians when they begin to sell their books. Many of the marketing schemes come very close to sin if they don't simply tumble over the edge into overt wrong behavior.

The Christian Guide to selling Online

Writing In InDesign Revised Edition 2.5

This updated my popular Writing In InDesign to include the capabilities of CS6. I started as a fine artist and then added 40 years of graphic design experieince. I now find that publishing books is a better creative thrill than any canvas or watercolor.

Writing In InDesign

www.ingramcontent.com/pod-product-compliance
Lightning Source LLC
Chambersburg PA
CBHW051223170526
45166CB00005B/2025